Table of C

Math Homewc
Grade

Balls of Fun

Use the Number Bank to write the correct number in each ball.

eight hundred fifty-two

_____

one thousand five hundred forty-three

_____

fifteen thousand eight hundred twenty-four

_____

nine thousand thirty-two

_____

forty-three thousand forty-one

_____

two thousand thirty

_____

seventeen thousand nine

_____

four thousand seven hundred twelve

_____

eighty-four thousand two hundred ten

_____

Unscramble the numbers to match the words in each ball.

7,421 _____

4,135 _____

41,820 _____

90,107 _____

10,434 _____

3,200 _____

2,093 _____

582 _____

41,285 _____

Number Bank

43,041	852	15,824	4,712	17,009
2,030	9,032	84,210	1,543	

©1993 Instructional Fair, Inc.

Puzzling Numbers

Use the clues to fill in the correct numbers in the puzzle below.

Across

1. 2 thousand 625
2. 3 thousand 42
5. 3 hundred twenty
6. 1 thousand ninety-two
8. 5 hundred eighty-one
10. 60 thousand 4 hundred
11. 78 thousand 9 hundred 1
13. 1 thousand ninety-one
15. 8 hundred 2
16. 55 thousand 5 hundred 23
17. 6 thousand 5 hundred twenty
19. nine hundred 83
20. 1 hundred eight
21. seven thousand 215
22. six hundred fifty-one

Down

1. 23 thousand fifty-six
2. 3 thousand 62
3. 4 thousand 2 hundred 1
4. 96 thousand 5 hundred 74
6. eleven thousand 367
7. 31 thousand two
9. twelve hundred 9
10. 61 thousand 2 hundred 53
12. 9 hundred 85
14. 13 thousand 2
15. 8 thousand 351
17. six hundred 32
18. 6 hundred ninety-five

5 ©1993 Instructional Fair, Inc.

Stack 'Em Up

Put each set of numbers in order from largest to smallest on the flag poles.

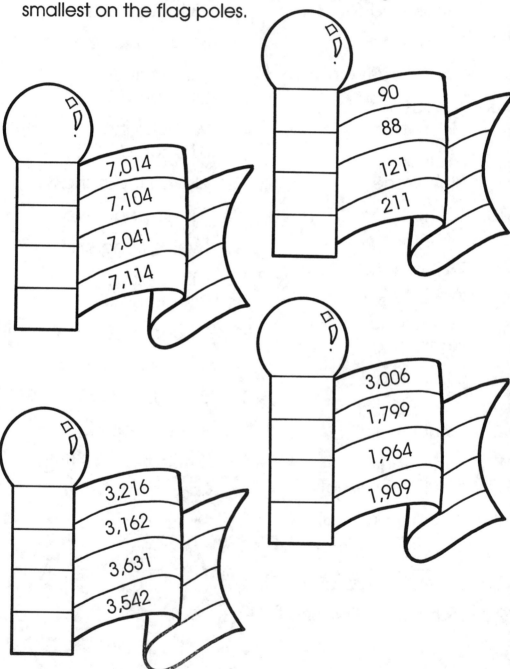

7,014
7,104
7,041
7,114

90
88
121
211

3,216
3,162
3,631
3,542

3,006
1,799
1,964
1,909

Color Comparison

If the answer is **<**, color the section red.

If the answer is **>**, color the section blue.

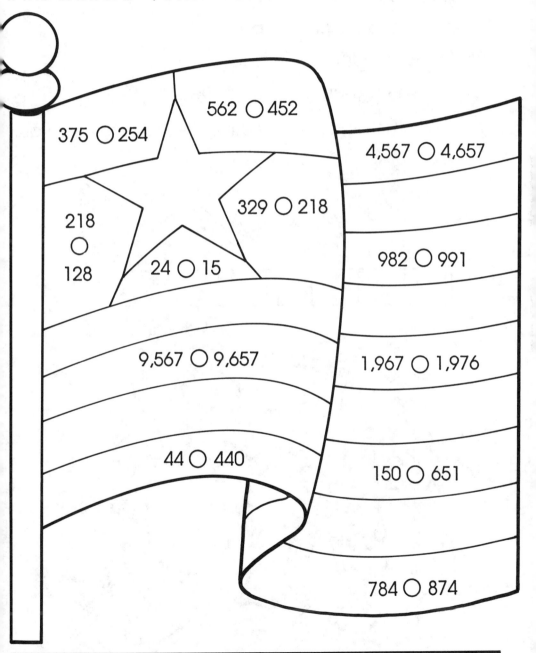

562 ◯ 452

375 ◯ 254

4,567 ◯ 4,657

218 ◯ 128

329 ◯ 218

982 ◯ 991

24 ◯ 15

9,567 ◯ 9,657

1,967 ◯ 1,976

44 ◯ 440

150 ◯ 651

784 ◯ 874

7 ©1993 Instructional Fair, Inc.

In the Right Place

Color the rectangles on page 9 using the clues below.

2 in the tens place - red

9 in the thousands place - purple

7 in the hundreds place - green

1 in the ten-thousands place - blue

Hint: Fill in the boxes below using the clues to help you.

97,102	91,000	17,902	16,500	8,602	4,655
655	2,674	118,543	10,000	985	844,964
4,044	1,545	315,000	13,612	986,243	8,401
752	37,777	107,651	301	79,671	99,562
5,761	8,763	42,034	87,964	29,002	9,852
700	95,704	395,001	22,981	9,404	109,000
27,156	827,961	24	3,627	6,666	27,900
428,671	8,234	20,021	1,022	900	2,643
98,151	62,004	7,028	827	38,657	22,070
29,000	39,444	134	5,000	762	1,700
249,142	9,543	8,497	93,641	2,754	95,761
59,102	49,000	304,000	987,132	80,740	6,702
47,877	8,654	413,650	11,652	4,560	7,290
982,148	21,001	917,250	217,950	8,640	8,000
8,008	67,841	12,400	15,852	60,971	21,907
821	33,124	4,891	600	627	1,427
1,020	329	464	7,900	3,424	41,222

My Place or Yours?

Fill in the boxes with the correct numbers using the clues below.

			millions			thousands		

5 in the thousands place

6 in the ones place

1 in the ten-millions place

3 in the hundreds place

2 in the millions place

7 in the tens place

9 in the hundred-millions place

0 in the ten-thousands place

4 in the hundred-thousands place

On the Right Path

Trace the path from start to finish that adds up to 150.

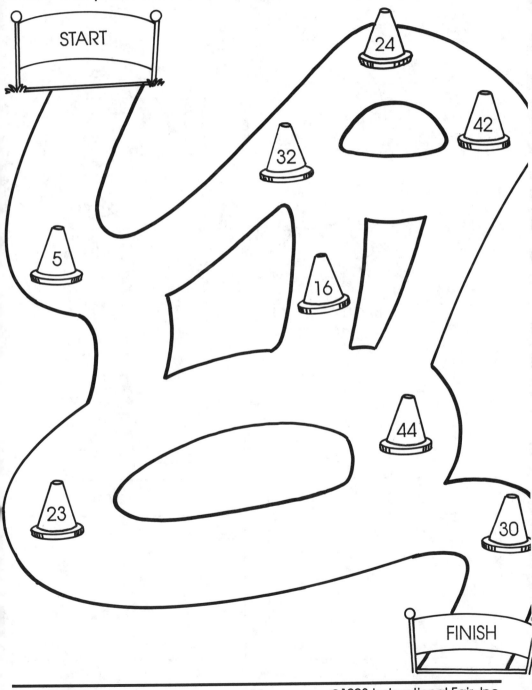

11

Shoot to Score!

Use 5 arrows to make the points given.

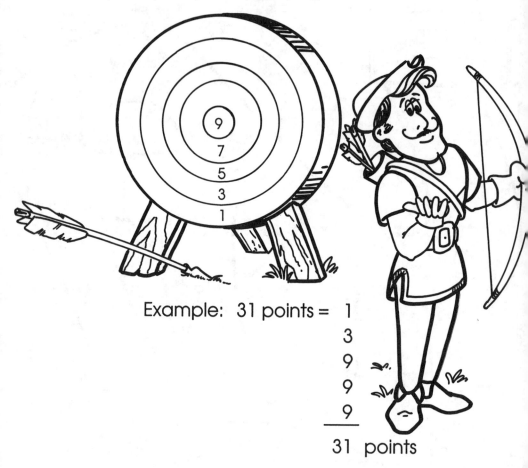

Example: 31 points =   1
                         3
                         9
                         9
                         9
                      —————
                         31 points

37 points	23 points

Using the target on page 12, use as many arrows as you choose to make . . .

47 points

97 points

Using each of the the targets below, make 100 points. But, use the least amount of arrows possible!

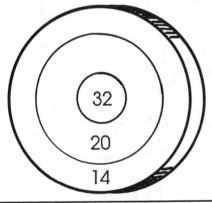

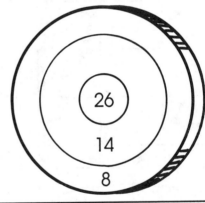

100 points

100 points

13   ©1993 Instructional Fair, Inc.

Line 'Em Up!

A Magic Square

Arrange the numbers in each hat so that the rows,
columns and diagonals have the same sum. Use the
Sum Bank on page 15 to help you.

Example:

8	1	6
3	5	7
4	9	2

sum = 15

Multiples of 2

sum = _____

2   16

8

10   18

12

4   6

14

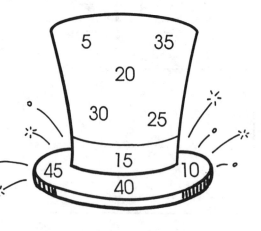

5   35

20

30   25

15

45   10

40

Multiples of 5

sum = _____

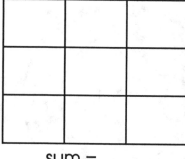

Odd numbers from 3 to 19

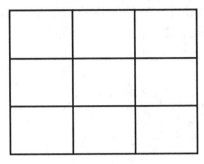

sum = _____

Even numbers from 30 to 46

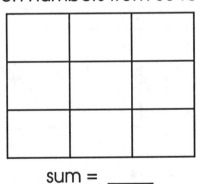

sum = _____

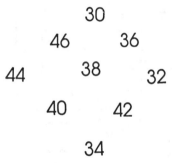

Sum Bank

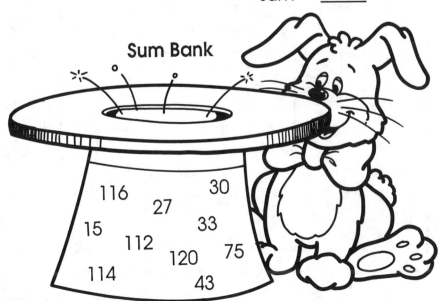

116   30
27
15   33
112   75
120
114   43

A "Maze"ing!

Follow the arrows through the maze. Fill in the circles as you go with numbers from the Number Bank. The first one has been done to get you started.

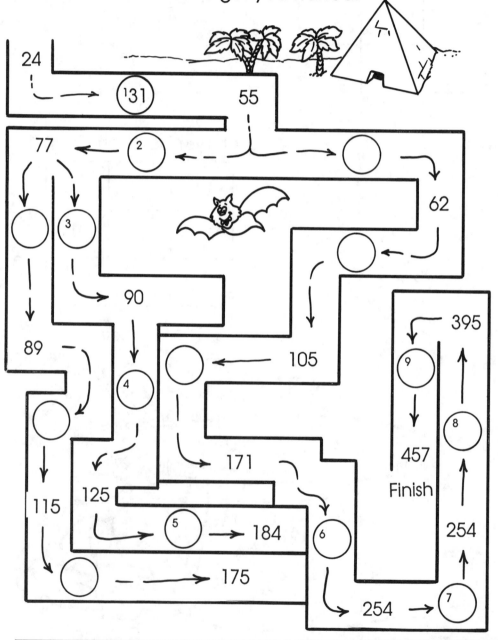

Number Bank

43 - W	26 - R	12 - Z	22 - A	66 - X
7 - Y	31 - M	59 - I	141 - U	13 - T
60 - E	83 - S	35 - H	62 - N	0 - F

Match the number and letter to reveal a secret message.

$$\frac{M}{1} \quad \frac{}{2} \quad \frac{}{3} \quad \frac{}{4}$$

$$\frac{}{5} \quad \frac{}{6}$$

$$\frac{}{7} \quad \frac{}{8} \quad \frac{}{9}$$

← THIS WAY

17 ©1993 Instructional Fair, Inc.

Oh My!

What should you do if you are surrounded by 20 lions, 15 tigers and 10 leopards?

To answer the riddle, solve the problems. Write the letter of the problem under the box that contains its answer. The first one has been done as an example.

W
$$\begin{array}{r} 269 \\ -\ 54 \\ \hline 215 \end{array}$$

O
$$\begin{array}{r} 34 \\ -\ 21 \\ \hline \end{array}$$

H
$$\begin{array}{r} 175 \\ -\ 18 \\ \hline \end{array}$$

T
$$\begin{array}{r} 78 \\ -\ 62 \\ \hline \end{array}$$

D
$$\begin{array}{r} 986 \\ -\ 22 \\ \hline \end{array}$$

F
$$\begin{array}{r} 723 \\ -\ 248 \\ \hline \end{array}$$

P
$$\begin{array}{r} 635 \\ -\ 356 \\ \hline \end{array}$$

R
$$\begin{array}{r} 84 \\ -\ 67 \\ \hline \end{array}$$

A
$$\begin{array}{r} 700 \\ -\ 526 \\ \hline \end{array}$$

G
$$\begin{array}{r} 635 \\ -\ 547 \\ \hline \end{array}$$

N
$$\begin{array}{r} 314 \\ -\ 246 \\ \hline \end{array}$$

U
$$\begin{array}{r} 546 \\ -\ 382 \\ \hline \end{array}$$

M	824 - 615
I	954 - 567
Y	947 - 682

S	743 - 651
J	489 - 293
E	167 - 93

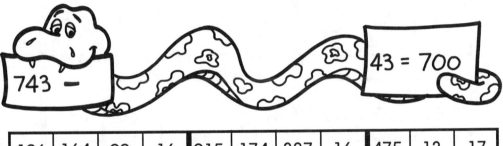

743 —

43 = 700

196	164	92	16	215	174	387	16	475	13	17
				W						

16	157	74	209	74	17	17	265	88	13

17	13	164	68	964	16	13	92	16	13	279

174	68	964	196	164	209	279	13	475	475

19 ©1993 Instructional Fair, Inc.

Tic-Tac-Toe Time

Solve the problems on page 21. Find the answers below and put an X on each of them. Put O's on all the other squares. Find the tic-tac-toes.

74	108	21
28	819	19
39	237	35

415	597	224
24	582	85
76	96	329

140	222	27
432	69	108
66	421	473

39	154	48
118	702	597
625	88	317

772	34	116
58	204	61
741	47	41

98	317	14
218	64	11
882	67	224

93 - 54	134 - 70	174 - 58	132 - 47
164 - 24	257 - 39	170 - 96	947 - 65
768 - 27	672 - 75	64 - 37	58 - 44
77 - 58	170 - 74	483 - 414	761 - 59
525 - 52	883 - 64	234 - 30	439 - 24

21 ©1993 Instructional Fair, Inc.

Seek and Circle

Solve the problems. Find the answers in the chart on page 23 and circle them. Answers are in a straight line, but can go in any direction.

5002 - 4310	7854 - 5319	1992 - 1564	8765 - 3201
7312 - 1003	4432 - 520	3989 - 2675	714 - 503
8341 - 3452	5452 - 2013	9861 - 3072	5971 - 1099
8600 - 7992	6834 - 683	7430 - 2467	3663 - 1988

5	3	5	2	4	0	5	3	2
9	7	2	4	3	9	0	7	1
0	4	1	7	8	5	6	0	1
7	3	3	4	7	0	6	3	9
1	0	5	7	5	5	6	4	2
5	9	6	3	0	9	8	9	3
2	7	8	4	2	2	1	0	8
0	7	2	5	1	4	8	5	3
8	9	5	9	9	3	1	2	5
6	3	8	7	3	4	6	0	4
3	8	2	9	7	0	7	6	4
4	4	9	3	4	3	5	9	4
9	7	0	4	5	9	8	5	7
1	5	1	6	9	4	3	0	9
3	9	7	0	2	9	8	7	6

23 ©1993 Instructional Fair, Inc.

Clowning Around

©1993 Instructional Fair, Inc.

Solve the problems. On page 24, color the spaces indicated by the problems using the answers in the Number Bank.

a
$$682$$
$$+ \ 195$$

b
$$852$$
$$- \ 49$$

c
$$624$$
$$+ \ 96$$

d
$$692$$
$$- \ 431$$

e
$$1152$$
$$- \ 483$$

f
$$2569$$
$$- \ 784$$

g

$$596$$
$$+ \ 281$$

Number Bank

red = 261	purple = 877
blue = 1,209	brown = 803
pink = 1,785	orange = 669
green = 394	yellow = 720

h

$$1496$$
$$- \ 287$$

i
$$1396$$
$$+ \ 389$$

j
$$1523$$
$$- \ 1129$$

k
$$785$$
$$- \ 391$$

l
$$243$$
$$+ \ 560$$

m
$$1296$$
$$- \ 419$$

n
$$679$$
$$+ \ 530$$

Magic Boxes

Fill in the missing numbers by subtracting across and subtracting down.

13	7	
5	2	

8	3	
	3	2

15		8
9		5

	8	8
7	1	

	13	21
	53	49

72		36
	25	
43		

Fill in the missing numbers by adding across and adding down.

5	6	
7	8	

8	1	
	5	11

9	5	
10		22

3		7
8		13

	66	79
	85	103

73		112
	65	
93		

On the Right Path

Complete the path by adding or subtracting. The first one has been done for you.

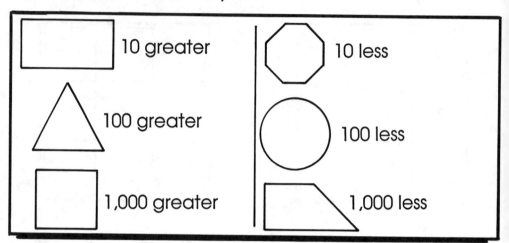

rectangle	10 greater	octagon	10 less
triangle	100 greater	circle	100 less
square	1,000 greater	trapezoid	1,000 less

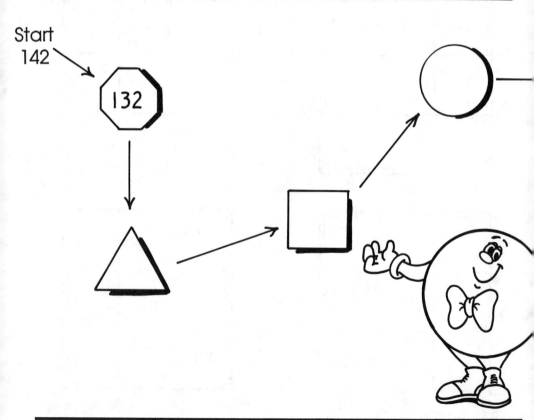

Start
142

132

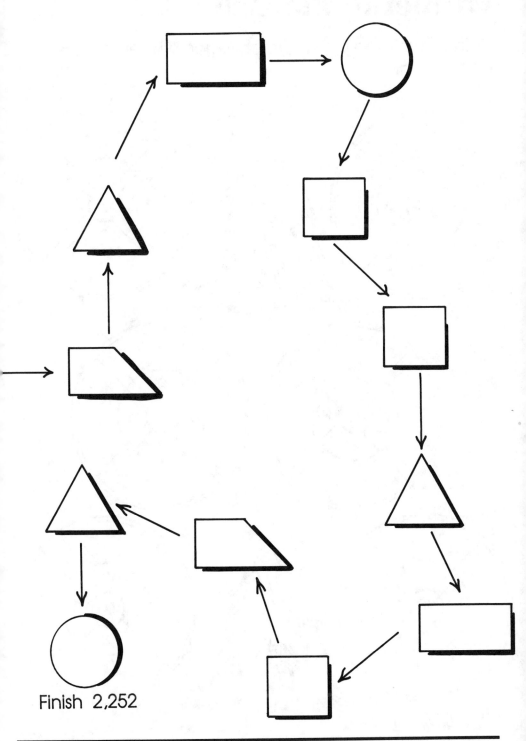

Finish 2,252

©1993 Instructional Fair, Inc.

Farmer in the Dell

Fill in the missing parts of the wagon wheels by multiplying.

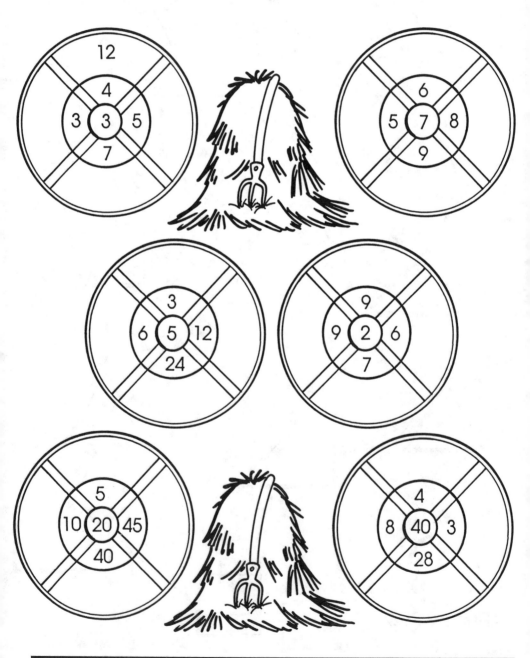

To find a farmer's famous expression, shade in the
multiples of:

3

13	24		2
		11	17
8	12	3	52
			68
29	27	88	61
70	18	30	10

5

88	50		91
			18
73	12	15	72	2
16	37	30	42
		45	13

6

11	72	54	33
		51	16
63	12		21
29	36	37	56
	61		
11	48		49
7		60	19

8

9		24	44
28	36		4
		88	68
33	83	64	85
	51		
58		56	57	23
	37		

9

4	72	81	3
25	18	42	49	19
		61	
67	99	89	45	5
		57	59	28
34	54	63	9

©1993 Instructional Fair, Inc.

The Key to Coloring

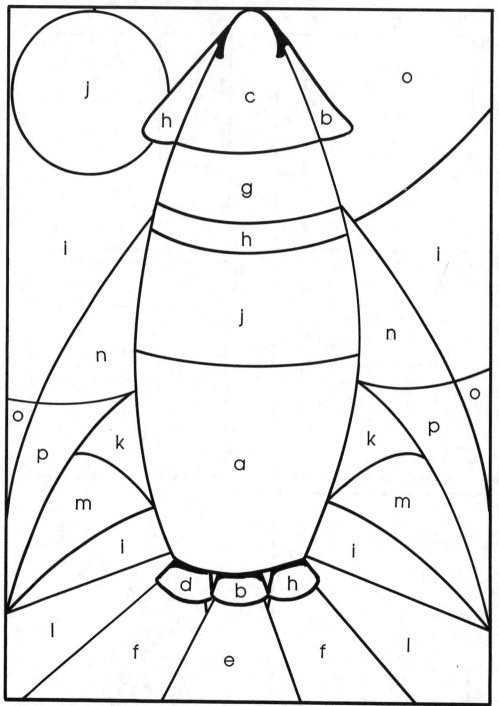

Solve the problems. On page 32, color the spaces indicated by the letters using the answers in the Number Bank.

a. 2 x 14   b. 9 x 4   c. 7 x 4   d. 6 x 6

e. 2 x 36   f. 9 x 8   g. 5 x 5   h. 1 x 36

i. 2 x 32   j. 4 x 5   k. 1 x 28   l. 0 x 32

m. 7 x 6   n. 9 x 9   o. 1 x 64   p. 2 x 10

Number Bank

0 = green	28 = purple	64 = green
20 = yellow	36 = black	72 = brown
25 = red	42 = orange	81 = gold

33 ©1993 Instructional Fair, Inc.

Solving the Riddles

Solve the problems to find the answer to this riddle:

> **What has a lot of legs and goes on picnics?**

U 64 × 53	G 28 × 49	L 21 × 94	R 48 × 76
T 56 × 83	N 45 × 36	A 38 × 47	H 54 × 72
Y 63 × 24	F 82 × 56	I 24 × 96	M 87 × 32

$$\overline{\text{1,786}} \quad\quad \overline{\text{3,888}} \;\; \overline{\text{3,392}} \;\; \overline{\text{1,620}} \;\; \overline{\text{1,372}} \;\; \overline{\text{3,648}} \;\; \overline{\text{1,512}}$$

$$\overline{\text{1,786}} \;\; \overline{\text{1,620}} \;\; \overline{\text{4,648}} \quad\quad \overline{\text{4,592}} \;\; \overline{\text{1,786}} \;\; \overline{\text{2,784}} \;\; \overline{\text{2,304}} \;\; \overline{\text{1,974}} \;\; \overline{\text{1,512}}$$

Solve the problems to find the answer to this riddle:

> **What do you call a knife that cuts four loaves of bread at once?**

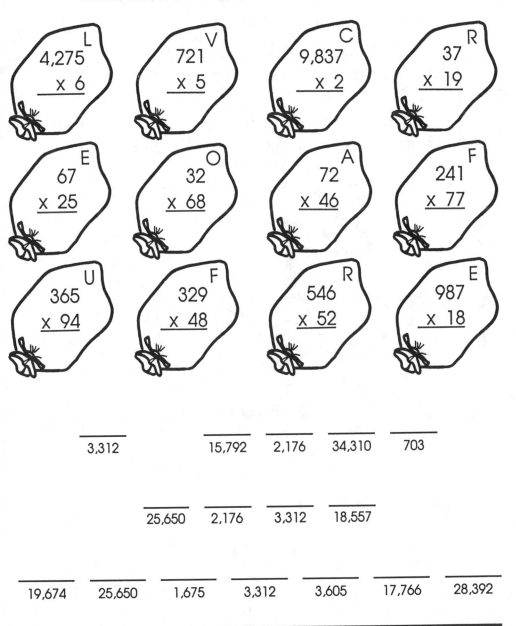

L 4,275 × 6	V 721 × 5	C 9,837 × 2	R 37 × 19
E 67 × 25	O 32 × 68	A 72 × 46	F 241 × 77
U 365 × 94	F 329 × 48	R 546 × 52	E 987 × 18

3,312	15,792	2,176	34,310	703

25,650	2,176	3,312	18,557

19,674	25,650	1,675	3,312	3,605	17,766	28,392

©1993 Instructional Fair, Inc.

Get a Clue!

Using the clues below, put the numbers above each problem in the ☐'s to get the correct answer.

Clues

- The product of two odd numbers is odd.
- A factor ending in 5 will have a product ending in 5 or 0.
- The product of two numbers cannot have more digits than the total number of digits in the two factors.

1.
```
    7 3 2
    7   2
  x     3
  ───────
    216
```

2.
```
    5 5 7
    ☐ ☐
  x   ☐
  ───────
    285
```

3.
```
    1 2 3 4
      ☐ ☐
  x   ☐ ☐
  ───────
    322
```

Tutor's Guide

This tutor's guide contains answer keys for Math Grade 4. Pull it out from the book to use as a guide.

Balls of Fun

Use the Number Bank to write the correct number in each ball.

- eight hundred fifty-two — **852**
- one thousand five hundred forty-three — **1,543**
- fifteen thousand eight hundred twenty-four — **15,824**
- nine thousand thirty-two — **9,032**
- forty-three thousand forty-one — **43,041**
- two thousand thirty — **2,030**
- seventeen thousand nine — **17,009**
- four thousand seven hundred twelve — **4,712**
- eighty-four thousand two hundred ten — **84,210**

Math IF0275   2   ©1993 Instructional Fair, Inc.

Whole Numbers

Unscramble the numbers to match the words in each ball.

- 7,421 — **4,712**
- 4,135 — **1,543**
- 41,820 — **84,210**
- 90,107 — **17,009**
- 10,434 — **43,041**
- 3,200 — **2,030**
- 2,093 — **9,032**
- 582 — **852**
- 41,285 — **15,824**

Number Bank

43,041	852	15,824	4,712	17,009
	2,030	9,032	84,210	1,543

Math IF0275   3   ©1993 Instructional Fair, Inc.

Puzzling Numbers

Whole Numbers

Use the clues to fill in the correct numbers in the puzzle below.

Across

1. 2 thousand 625
2. 3 thousand 42
5. 3 hundred twenty
6. 1 thousand ninety-two
8. 5 hundred eighty-one
10. 60 thousand 4 hundred
11. 78 thousand 9 hundred 1
13. 1 thousand ninety-one
15. 8 hundred 2
16. 55 thousand 5 hundred 23
17. 6 thousand 5 hundred twenty
19. nine hundred 83
20. 1 hundred eight
21. seven thousand 215
22. six hundred fifty-one

Down

1. 23 thousand fifty-six
2. 3 thousand 62
3. 4 thousand 2 hundred 1
4. 96 thousand 5 hundred 74
6. eleven thousand 367
7. 31 thousand two
9. twelve hundred 9
10. 61 thousand 2 hundred 53
12. 9 hundred 85
14. 13 thousand 2
15. 8 thousand 351
17. six hundred 32
18. 6 hundred ninety-five

Math IF0275   5   ©1993 Instructional Fair, Inc.

Stack 'Em Up

Put each set of numbers in order from largest to smallest on the flag poles.

7,014	90	3,006	3,216
7,104	88	1,799	3,162
7,041	121	1,964	3,631
7,114	211	1,909	3,542

- Pole 1: **7114, 7104, 7041, 7014**
- Pole 2: **211, 121, 90, 88**
- Pole 3: **3006, 1964, 1909, 1799**
- Pole 4: **3631, 3542, 3216, 3162**

Math IF0275   6   ©1993 Instructional Fair, Inc.

Color Comparison

Comparing Numbers

If the answer is <, color the section red.
If the answer is >, color the section blue.

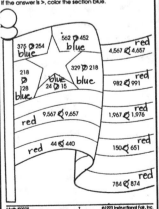

- 562 > 452 — **blue**
- 375 > 254 — **blue**
- 4,567 < 4,657 — **red**
- 329 > 218 — **blue**
- 218 > 128 — **blue**
- 24 > 15 — **blue**
- 982 < 991 — **red**
- 9,567 < 9,657 — **red**
- 1,967 < 1,976 — **red**
- 44 < 440 — **red**
- 150 < 651 — **red**
- 784 < 874 — **red**

Math IF0275   7   ©1993 Instructional Fair, Inc.

In the Right Place

Color the rectangles on page 9 using the clues below.

2 in the tens place - red
9 in the thousands place - purple
7 in the hundreds place - green
1 in the ten-thousands place - blue

Hint: Fill in the boxes below using the clues to help you.

ten-thousands	thousands	hundreds	tens	ones
1	9	7	2	

Math IF0275   8   ©1993 Instructional Fair, Inc.

Place Value

97,102	91,000	14,992 blue	114,509 blue	8,602	4,655
655	2,674	148,545 blue	10,800 blue	985	844,964
4,044	1,545	319,000 blue	13,412 blue	986,243	8,401
762 green	37,777 green	107,651	301	79,671 purple	99,562 purple
6,761 green	8,763 green	42,034	87,964	29,002 purple	9,852 purple
700 green	95,704 green	395,001	22,981	9,664 purple	109,000 purple
27,156	827,961		24 red	3,621 blue	6,666	27,900
428,671	8,234	20,081 red	1,022 red	900	2,643
98,151	62,004	7,028 red	8971 red	38,657	12,070
29,000 purple	39,444 purple	134	5,000	762 green	1,700 green
249,162 purple	2,764 purple	8,497	93,641	2,764 green	36,761 green
59,162 purple	69,000 purple	304,000	987,132	80,740 green	6,702 green
47,877	8,654	94,992 blue	9,662 blue	4,560	7,290
982,148	21,001	87,250 blue	21,992 blue	8,640	8,000
8,008	67,841	12,400 blue	16,852 blue	60,971	21,907
821 red	33,128 red	4,891	600	621 red	128 red
1,022 red	329 red	464	7,900	3,428 red	41,221 red

Math IF0275   9   ©1993 Instructional Fair, Inc.

My Place or Yours?

Place Value

Fill in the boxes with the correct numbers using the clues below.

millions			thousands				
9	1	2	4	0	5	3	7	6

5 in the thousands place
6 in the ones place
1 in the ten-millions place
3 in the hundreds place
2 in the millions place
7 in the tens place
9 in the hundred-millions place
0 in the ten-thousands place
4 in the hundred-thousands place

Math IF0275   10   ©1993 Instructional Fair, Inc.

On the Right Path

Addition

Trace the path from start to finish that adds up to 150.

START
24
42
32
5
16
44
23
30
FINISH

Math IF0275   11   ©1993 Instructional Fair, Inc.

Shoot to Score!

Use 5 arrows to make the points given.

Example: 31 points =
1
3
9
9
9
31 points

Answers will vary.

37 points
9
9
9
+5
37

23 points
5
5
5
+ 3
23

Math IF0275   12   ©1993 Instructional Fair, Inc.

Addition

Using the target on page 12, use as many arrows as you choose to make . . .

47 points
9
9
9
5
5
+5 = 47

97 points
9 5 7
9 5 7
9 5 7
9 5 7
5 5 13 = 97

Using each of the targets below, make 100 points. But, use the least amount of arrows possible!

32 20 14

26 114 8

100 points
32
14
14
20
+20
100

100 points
26
26
26
14
+ 8
100

Math IF0275   13   ©1993 Instructional Fair, Inc.

Line 'Em Up!

A Magic Square

Arrange the numbers in each hat so that the rows, columns and diagonals have the same sum. Use the Sum Bank on page 15 to help you.

Example:

8	1	6
3	5	7
4	9	2

sum = 15

Multiples of 2

16	2	12
6	10	14
8	18	4

sum = 30

2 16
8
10 18
12
14

Multiples of 5

40	5	30
15	25	35
20	45	10

sum = 75

5 35
20
30 25
15
45 40 10

Math IF0275   14   ©1993 Instructional Fair, Inc.

Addition

Odd numbers from 3 to 19

17	3	13
7	11	15
9	19	5

sum = 33

17
3 13
11 9
19 15
5

Even numbers from 30 to 46

44	30	40
34	38	42
36	46	32

sum = 114

30
46 36
44 38 32
40 42
34

Sum Bank

116 30
27
15 112 33
120 75
114 43

Math IF0275   15   ©1993 Instructional Fair, Inc.

A "Maze"ing!

Follow the arrows through the maze. Fill in the circles as you go with numbers from the Number Bank. The first one has been done to get you started.

START
24
31
55
77
32
7
12 13
62
43
90
105
89
395
44
85
26
171
457
125
Finish
59 184
83
60 175
254
254
D

Math IF0275   16   ©1993 Instructional Fair, Inc.

Addition

Number Bank				
43 - W	26 - R	12 - Z	22 - A	66 - X
7 - Y	31 - M	59 - I	141 - U	13 - T
60 - E	83 - S	35 - H	62 - N	0 - F

Match the number and letter to reveal a secret message.

M   A   T   H
1   2   3   4

I   S
5   6

F   U   N
7   8   9

← THIS WAY

Math IF0275   17   ©1993 Instructional Fair, Inc.

Oh My!

What should you do if you are surrounded by 20 lions, 15 tigers and 10 leopards?

To answer the riddle, solve the problems. Write the letter of the problem under the box that contains its answer. The first one has been done as an example.

W	269 - 54 215	O	34 - 21 13	H	175 - 18 157
T	78 - 62 16	D	986 - 22 964	F	723 - 248 475
P	635 - 356 279	R	84 - 67 17	A	700 - 526 174
G	635 - 547 88	N	314 - 246 68	U	546 - 382 164

Math IF0275   18   ©1993 Instructional Fair, Inc.

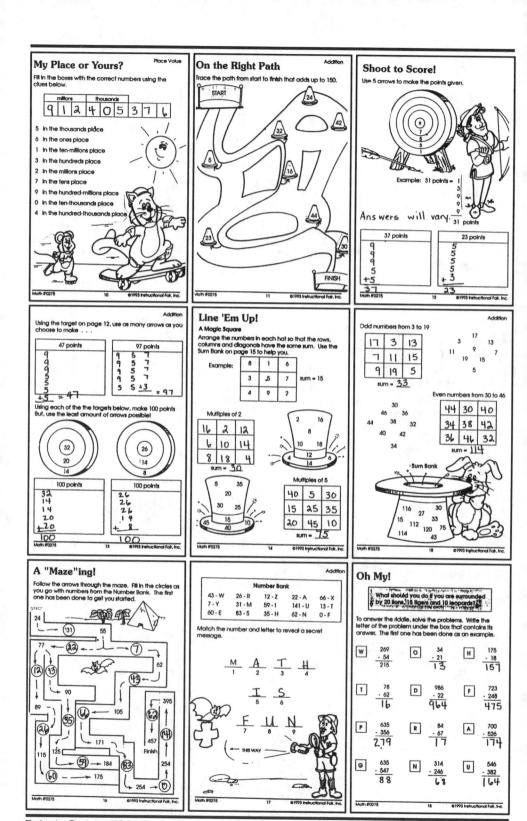

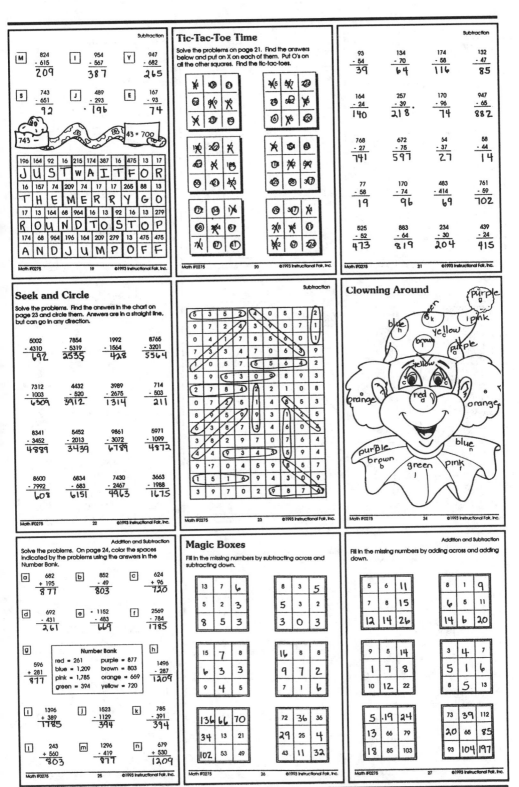

Subtraction (page 19)

M 824 − 615 = 209	I 954 − 567 = 387	Y 947 − 682 = 265
S 743 − 651 = 92	J 489 − 293 = 196	E 167 − 93 = 74

743 − __43 = 700

196	164	92	16	215	174	387	16	475	13	17
J	U	S	T	W	A	I	T	F	O	R

16	157	74	209	74	17	17	265	88	13
T	H	E	M	E	R	R	Y	G	O

17	13	164	68	964	16	13	92	16	13	279
R	O	U	N	D	T	O	S	T	O	P

174	68	964	196	164	209	279	13	475	475
A	N	D	J	U	M	P	O	F	F

Math IF0275   19   ©1993 Instructional Fair, Inc.

Tic-Tac-Toe Time (page 20)

Solve the problems on page 21. Find the answers below and put an X on each of them. Put O's on all the other squares. Find the tic-tac-toes.

Math IF0275   20   ©1993 Instructional Fair, Inc.

Subtraction (page 21)

93 − 54 = 39	134 − 70 = 64	174 − 58 = 116	132 − 47 = 85
164 − 24 = 140	257 − 39 = 218	170 − 96 = 74	947 − 65 = 882
768 − 27 = 741	672 − 75 = 597	54 − 37 = 27	58 − 44 = 14
77 − 58 = 19	170 − 74 = 96	483 − 414 = 69	761 − 59 = 702
525 − 52 = 473	883 − 64 = 819	234 − 30 = 204	439 − 24 = 415

Math IF0275   21   ©1993 Instructional Fair, Inc.

Seek and Circle (page 22)

Solve the problems. Find the answers in the chart on page 23 and circle them. Answers are in a straight line, but can go in any direction.

5002 − 4310 = 692	7854 − 5319 = 2535	1992 − 1564 = 428	8765 − 3201 = 5564
7312 − 1003 = 6309	4432 − 520 = 3912	3989 − 2675 = 1314	714 − 503 = 211
8341 − 3452 = 4889	5452 − 2013 = 3439	9861 − 3072 = 6789	5971 − 1099 = 4872
8600 − 7992 = 608	6834 − 683 = 6151	7430 − 2467 = 4963	3663 − 1988 = 1675

Math IF0275   22   ©1993 Instructional Fair, Inc.

Subtraction (page 23)

Math IF0275   23   ©1993 Instructional Fair, Inc.

Clowning Around (page 24)

Math IF0275   24   ©1993 Instructional Fair, Inc.

Addition and Subtraction (page 25)

Solve the problems. On page 24, color the spaces indicated by the problems using the answers in the Number Bank.

a 682 + 195 = 877	b 852 − 49 = 803	c 624 + 96 = 720
d 692 − 431 = 261	e 1152 − 483 = 669	f 2569 − 784 = 1785
g 596 + 281 = 877		h 1496 − 287 = 1209

Number Bank
red = 261   purple = 877
blue = 1,209   brown = 803
pink = 1,785   orange = 669
green = 394   yellow = 720

i 1396 + 389 = 1785	j 1523 − 1129 = 394	k 785 − 391 = 394
l 243 + 560 = 803	m 1296 − 419 = 877	n 679 + 530 = 1209

Math IF0275   25   ©1993 Instructional Fair, Inc.

Magic Boxes (page 26)

Fill in the missing numbers by subtracting across and subtracting down.

13	7	6
5	2	3
8	5	3

8	3	5
5	3	2
3	0	3

15	7	8
6	3	3
9	4	5

16	8	8
9	7	2
7	1	6

136	66	70
34	13	21
102	53	49

72	36	36
29	25	4
43	11	32

Math IF0275   26   ©1993 Instructional Fair, Inc.

Addition and Subtraction (page 27)

Fill in the missing numbers by adding across and adding down.

5	6	11
7	8	15
12	14	26

8	1	9
6	5	11
14	6	20

9	5	14
1	7	8
10	12	22

3	4	7
5	1	6
8	5	13

5	19	24
13	66	79
18	85	103

73	39	112
20	65	85
93	104	197

Math IF0275   27   ©1993 Instructional Fair, Inc.

Tutor's Guide IF0275   C   ©1993 Instructional Fair, Inc.

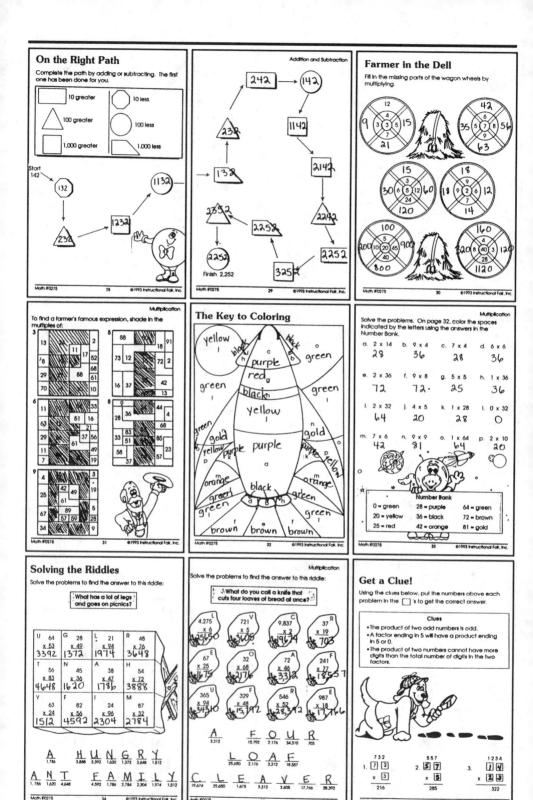

On the Right Path

Complete the path by adding or subtracting. The first one has been done for you.

- ☐ 10 greater
- △ 100 greater
- ▭ 1,000 greater
- ⬡ 10 less
- ◯ 100 less
- ▱ 1,000 less

Start 142 → ⬡ 132 → ▭ 1232 → △ 238 → ◯ 1132

Addition and Subtraction

242 → 142 → 1142 → 2142
△ 238
▭ 132 → 2352 → 2252 → 2242 → 2252
◯ 2252
Finish 2,252 3252

Farmer in the Dell

Fill in the missing parts of the wagon wheels by multiplying.

Math IF0275   28   ©1993 Instructional Fair, Inc.
Math IF0275   29   ©1993 Instructional Fair, Inc.
Math IF0275   30   ©1993 Instructional Fair, Inc.

Multiplication

To find a farmer's famous expression, shade in the multiples of:

The Key to Coloring

Multiplication

Solve the problems. On page 32, color the spaces indicated by the letters using the answers in the Number Bank.

- a. 2 x 14 = 28
- b. 9 x 4 = 36
- c. 7 x 4 = 28
- d. 6 x 6 = 36
- e. 2 x 36 = 72
- f. 9 x 8 = 72
- g. 5 x 5 = 25
- h. 1 x 36 = 36
- i. 2 x 32 = 64
- j. 4 x 5 = 20
- k. 1 x 28 = 28
- l. 0 x 32 = 0
- m. 7 x 6 = 42
- n. 9 x 9 = 81
- o. 1 x 64 = 64
- p. 2 x 10 = 20

Number Bank
- 0 = green
- 20 = yellow
- 25 = red
- 28 = purple
- 36 = black
- 42 = orange
- 64 = green
- 72 = brown
- 81 = gold

Math IF0275   31   ©1993 Instructional Fair, Inc.
Math IF0275   32   ©1993 Instructional Fair, Inc.
Math IF0275   33   ©1993 Instructional Fair, Inc.

Solving the Riddles

Solve the problems to find the answer to this riddle:

What has a lot of legs and goes on picnics?

U	G	L	R
64 x 53 = 3392	28 x 49 = 1372	21 x 94 = 1974	48 x 76 = 3648
T	N	A	H
56 x 83 = 4648	45 x 36 = 1620	38 x 47 = 1786	54 x 72 = 3888
Y	F	I	M
63 x 24 = 1512	82 x 56 = 4592	24 x 96 = 2304	87 x 32 = 2784

A N T   H U N G R Y   A N T   F A M I L Y

Multiplication

Solve the problems to find the answer to this riddle:

What do you call a knife that cuts four loaves of bread at once?

- L 4,275 x 6 = 25,650
- V 721 x 5 = 3,605
- C 9,837 x 2 = 19,674
- R 37 x 19 = 703
- E 67 x 25 = 1,675
- F 32 x 68 = 2,176
- A 72 x 46 = 3,312
- 241 x 77 = 18,557
- U 365 x 94 = 34,310
- A 329 x 48 = 15,792
- 546 x 52 = 28,392
- 987 x 18 = 17,766

A F O U R   L O A F   C L E A V E R

Get a Clue!

Using the clues below, put the numbers above each problem in the ☐'s to get the correct answer.

Clues
- The product of two odd numbers is odd.
- A factor ending in 5 will have a product ending in 5 or 0.
- The product of two numbers cannot have more digits than the total number of digits in the two factors.

1. 732
   ☐☐x☐ = 216

2. 557
   ☐☐x☐ = 285

3. 1234
   ☐☐x☐☐ = 322

Math IF0275   34   ©1993 Instructional Fair, Inc.
Math IF0275   35   ©1993 Instructional Fair, Inc.
Math IF0275   36   ©1993 Instructional Fair, Inc.

Tutor's Guide IF0275   D   ©1993 Instructional Fair, Inc.

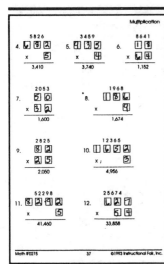

4. 5826 ☐☐☐ x ☐5 = 3,410

5. 3459 ☐☐☐☐ x ☐4 = 3,740

6. 8641 ☐☐ x ☐☐ = 1,152

7. 2053 ☐☐ x ☐☐ = 1,600

8. 1968 ☐☐☐☐ x ☐4 = 1,674

9. 2825 ☐☐ x ☐☐ = 2,050

10. 12365 ☐☐☐☐☐ x ☐ = 4,956

11. 52298 ☐☐☐☐☐ x ☐ = 41,460

12. 25674 ☐☐☐ x ☐☐ = 33,858

Math IF0275   37   ©1993 Instructional Fair, Inc.

Division Design

Color in the squares that have numbers divisible by 3, 4 or 7 to form a design.

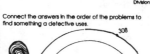

Put an X on the squares that are divisible by 5.
Put a △ on the squares that are divisible by 2.

Math IF0275   38   ©1993 Instructional Fair, Inc.

Make a design in the grid below. Write the numbers divisible by 5, 7 or 9 in the squares that will form a design. Then, fill in the other squares with numbers that are not divisible by 5, 7 or 9.

Math IF0275   39   ©1993 Instructional Fair, Inc.

Missing Pieces

Fill in the boxes with the missing numbers.

Math IF0275   40   ©1993 Instructional Fair, Inc.

Connect the answers in the order of the problems to find something a detective uses.

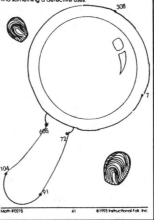

Math IF0275   41   ©1993 Instructional Fair, Inc.

Division in Space

Solve the problems. Then, connect the answers in the order of the problems to make a "space"tacular object! Note: You can only go to each number once.

1. $9\overline{)45}$ = 5
2. $5\overline{)15}$ = 3
3. $3\overline{)12}$ = 4
4. $6\overline{)36}$ = 6
5. $3\overline{)21}$ = 7
6. $6\overline{)48}$ = 8
7. $3\overline{)6}$ = 2
8. $3\overline{)27}$ = 9
9. $4\overline{)28}$ = 7
10. $2\overline{)10}$ = 5
11. $9\overline{)36}$ = 4
12. $2\overline{)18}$ = 9
13. $5\overline{)30}$ = 6
14. $6\overline{)18}$ = 3
15. $3\overline{)3}$ = 1
16. $5\overline{)40}$ = 8
17. $4\overline{)16}$ = 4
18. $7\overline{)49}$ = 7
19. $9\overline{)45}$ = 5
20. $8\overline{)72}$ = 9
21. $7\overline{)42}$ = 6

Math IF0275   42   ©1993 Instructional Fair, Inc.

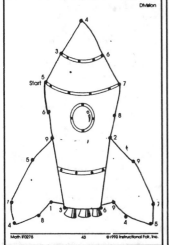

Math IF0275   43   ©1993 Instructional Fair, Inc.

A Fun Riddle

Solve the problems. Then, use the decoder to answer the riddle.

What is black, white and red all over?

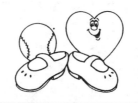

167 r3	308 r2	20 r2	358 r1	205 r2
U	H	A	S	T

7 r2	134 r3	51 r4	314 r3	52 r5
N	R	I	K	W

Math IF0275   44   ©1993 Instructional Fair, Inc.

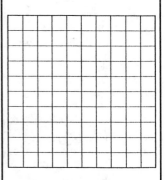

(could it be. Space Men from... Mars?)

$7\overline{)142}$ = 20 r 2   A

$2\overline{)717}$ = 358 r1 S
$9\overline{)2829}$ = 314 r3 K
$4\overline{)671}$ = 167 r3 U
$5\overline{)37}$ = 7 r2 N
$7\overline{)2201}$ = 314 r3 K

$8\overline{)421}$ = 52 r5 W
$7\overline{)361}$ = 51 r4 I
$3\overline{)617}$ = 205 r2 T
$3\overline{)926}$ = 308 r2 H
$4\overline{)82}$ = 20 r 2 A

$5\overline{)673}$ = 134 r3 R
$5\overline{)102}$ = 20 r2 A
$6\overline{)2149}$ = 358 r1 S
$8\overline{)2466}$ = 308 r2 H

Math IF0275   45   ©1993 Instructional Fair, Inc.

Math by Design

Solve the problems. Shade in each box that contains an answer. Write what geometric design you see.

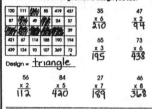

Design = triangle

56 x 2	84 x 5	27 x 7	46 x 8
112	420	189	368

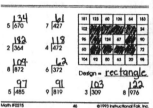

134 5)670	61 7)427
192 2)364	118 4)472
109 8)872	62 6)372

Design = rectangle

| 97 5)485 | 91 9)819 | 103 3)309 | 122 8)976 |

Math IF0275   46   ©1993 Instructional Fair, Inc.

Multiplication and Division

Design = square

140 7)980	56 x 8 448
73 438	287 x 3 861
82 492	224 672	38 x 9 342	812 9)7308
195 5)975	234 4)936	54 6)324	82 8)656

| 63 x 7 441 | 82 x 7 574 |

| 53 4)212 | 74 6)444 |

Design = parallelogram

| 25 x 3 75 | 76 x 4 304 | 15 9)135 | 49 8)392 |

Math IF0275   47   ©1993 Instructional Fair, Inc.

Solve and Search

Solve the problems below and on page 49. Then, find and circle the answers on the chart on page 49. Answers will be in a straight line, but may be in any direction.

1. 356 x 65 = 23,140
2. 1892 + 3567 = 5,459
3. 4562 - 384 = 4,178
4. 94 5)470
5. 1495 + 4582 = 6,077
6. 842 r 2 7)5896
7. 842 x 25 = 21,050
8. 2489 - 1956 = 533
9. 4876 + 542 = 5418
10. 140 7)980
11. 9821 - 6154 = 3,667
12. 645 x 72 = 46,440

Math IF0275   48   ©1993 Instructional Fair, Inc.

Review +, -, x, ÷

13. 9732 - 1871 = 7,861
14. 984 + 76 = 1,060
15. 83 9)747

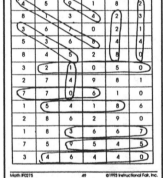

Math IF0275   49   ©1993 Instructional Fair, Inc.

Find the Sign

Write the correct sign in each circle to make the problem correct.

5 ⊗ 5 = 25

10 ⊕ 2 = 12

6 ⊗ 3 = 18

21 ⊖ 9 = 12

32 ⊖ 12 = 20

63 ⊖ 9 = 7

40 ⊕ 32 = 72

16 ⊗ 12 = 192

20 ⊘ 4 = 5

336 ⊕ 6 = 56

68 ⊕ 52 = 120

840 ⊖ 54 = 786

129 ⊘ 43 = 3

657 ⊖ 164 = 493

45 ⊗ 5 = 225

14 ⊗ 7 = 98

192 ⊕ 23 = 215

8 ⊗ 8 = 64

328 ⊘ 82 = 4

154 ⊖ 62 = 92

36 ⊖ 5 = 31

32 ⊘ 4 = 8

987 ⊘ 21 = 47

523 ⊕ 334 = 857

Math IF0275   50   ©1993 Instructional Fair, Inc.

Shaping Up

Use the shapes to solve the problems.

8	96	48
12	6	36
64	81	72

48 ⊕ 51 = 99   96 ÷ 8 = 12

12 x 48 = 576   51 - 36 = 15

64 ÷ 8 = 8   12 x 8 = 96

36 + 72 = 108   6 + 48 = 54

96 ÷ 6 = 16   64 x 72 = 4,608

72 ÷ 8 ⊘ 6 ⊕ 96 - 36 = 82

Math IF0275   51   ©1993 Instructional Fair, Inc.

Up We Go

Draw a straight line to match each number on the left with its rounded number on the right. Put the letters without lines through them on the blanks on page 53 to spell out a message.

Round to the nearest ten.

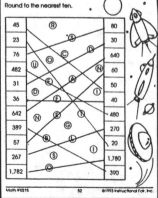

Math IF0275   52   ©1993 Instructional Fair, Inc.

Rounding

Round to the nearest hundred.

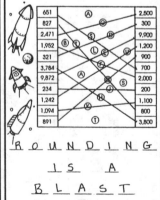

R O U N D I N G

I S   A

B L A S T

Math IF0275   53   ©1993 Instructional Fair, Inc.

Decimal Dilemma

Write each decimal. Then, shade in the answers on page 55 to find the answer to this riddle:

What are the two favorite letters of children?

1. six and ninety-one hundredths 6.91
2. three and five tenths 3.5
3. eight and twenty-four hundredths 8.24
4. four and three tenths 4.3
5. seven and thirty-six hundredths 7.36
6. eight and eighteen hundredths 8.18
7. two and one tenth 2.1
8. sixty and four hundredths 60.04
9. one hundredth .01
10. thirty-three and thirty-three hundredths 33.33
11. sixty-four and five tenths 64.5
12. four and seventy-five hundredths 4.75
13. nine and four hundredths 9.04
14. twenty-one and three tenths 21.3
15. fifty-six and forty-seven hundredths 56.47
16. seventy and five hundredths 70.05

Math IF0275   54   ©1993 Instructional Fair, Inc.

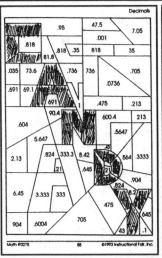

Tic-Tac-Toe with X and O

Solve the problems. Find the answers in the Answer Box and place either an X or an O in the square. Find the tic-tac-toes!

36.14 + 2.63 **38.77** X	59.16 + 3.04 **62.20** X	7.04 + 3.54 **10.58** O
67.50 + 51.04 **118.54** X	32.14 + 57.02 **89.16** X	82.73 + 27.67 **110.40** O
72.4 + 51.3 **123.7** O	12.57 + 3.41 **15.98** O	89.31 + 43.45 **132.76** X

43.67 - 32.98 **10.69** O	98.7 - 6.5 **92.2** O	72.04 - 3.43 **68.61** X
80.54 - 37.62 **42.92** X	42.4 - 14.3 **28.1** O	24.98 - 9.04 **15.94** O
36.72 - 5.98 **30.74** O	59.34 - 42.95 **16.39** O	82.47 - 3.95 **78.52** X

Answer Box

92.2 O	62.20 X	10.69 O	118.54 X	60.97 X
68.61 X	15.98 O	23.56 X	51.1 O	78.52 X	16.39 X
15.94 O	38.77 X	110.40 O	86.81 O	89.16 X
10.58 O	19.38 X	28.1 O	104.34 X	66.97 O	123.7 O
42.92 X	30.74 O	132.76 X	15.33 O	40.3 O

48.32 + 38.49 **86.81** O	32.4 + 7.9 **40.3** O	67.31 - 51.98 **15.33** X
27.51 - 3.95 **23.56** X	97.32 + 7.02 **104.34** O	55.5 - 4.4 **51.1** O
33.04 + 27.93 **60.97** X	78.42 - 59.04 **19.38** X	61.04 + 5.93 **66.97** X

Chow Time

Hamburger $1.20
  with cheese .... .20
Hot Dog .... .75
  with cheese .... .20
  with chili .... .20
French Fries .... .90
                    S   M   L
Soft Drink .... .75 .90 1.20

Fill in the missing numbers on the chart.

You Had	You Bought	Money Left Over
$3.75	1 cheeseburger 1 French fry 1 medium soft drink	$.55
$1.82	1 chili dog 1 small soft drink	$.12
$3.56	1 hamburger 1 cheese dog 1 small soft drink	$.66
$6.64	1 hamburger 1 chili cheese dog 2 French fries 1 small soft drink 1 medium soft drink	$.84
$5.96	1 cheeseburger 2 French fries 1 large soft drink	$1.56
$4.00	1 hamburger 1 French fry 1 large soft drink	$.70

Fractions of Pizzas

Using the Word Bank, write the fraction of the pizza that has been eaten. Then, circle the answers in the puzzle.

three-fourths   one-fourth   whole

one-third   one-sixth   three-fifths

five-eighths   one-half   six-tenths

four-tenths   two-thirds   one-fifth

Word Bank

two-thirds	one-fifth	six-tenths
three-fourths	one-fourth	one-sixth
five-eighths	whole	four-tenths
one-half	three-fifths	one-third

Wheels of Wonder

Fill in the missing blanks by adding the fractions from the inside out.

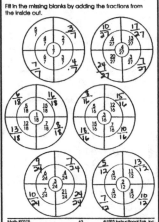

Way Up There!

Work the problems. Shade in the answers on kite A or B to see which kite went the highest.

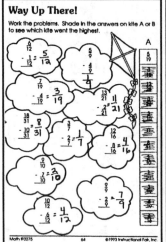

A

$\frac{6}{12} - \frac{1}{12} = \frac{5}{12}$

$\frac{5}{9} - \frac{4}{9} = \frac{1}{9}$

$\frac{7}{19} - \frac{4}{19} = \frac{3}{19}$

$\frac{18}{31} - \frac{10}{31} = \frac{8}{31}$

$\frac{13}{21} - \frac{11}{21} = \frac{11}{21}$

$\frac{2}{7} - \frac{1}{7} = \frac{1}{7}$

$\frac{12}{16} - \frac{8}{16} = \frac{4}{16}$

$\frac{9}{10} - \frac{7}{10} = \frac{3}{10}$

$\frac{9}{9} - \frac{2}{9} = \frac{7}{9}$

$\frac{10}{12} - \frac{6}{12} = \frac{4}{12}$

$\frac{5}{19}$

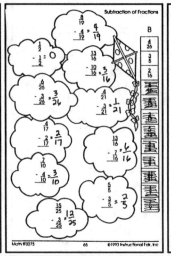

Subtraction of Fractions

B

$\frac{8}{19} - \frac{4}{19} = \frac{4}{19}$

$\frac{7}{7} - \frac{5}{7} = O$

$\frac{13}{16} - \frac{10}{16} = \frac{3}{16}$

$\frac{6}{26} - \frac{3}{26} = \frac{3}{26}$

$\frac{13}{21} - \frac{7}{21} = \frac{6}{21}$

$\frac{4}{17} - \frac{2}{17} = \frac{2}{17}$

$\frac{7}{10} - \frac{4}{10} = \frac{3}{10}$

$\frac{13}{16} - \frac{7}{16} = \frac{6}{16}$

$\frac{5}{5} - \frac{3}{5} = \frac{2}{5}$

$\frac{15}{25} - \frac{3}{25} = \frac{12}{25}$

$\frac{4}{26}$ $\frac{3}{5}$ $\frac{2}{16}$

TV Time

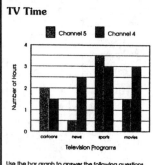

Channel 5 Channel 4

Use the bar graph to answer the following questions.

1. How many more hours does Channel 4 deliver televised news than Channel 5? **2 hours**
2. How many more hours does Channel 5 televise sports than Channel 4? **½ hour**
3. What is the total number of hours that Channel 5 televises news and cartoons? **2½ hours**

Graphing

4. How many more minutes of cartoons are televised by Channel 5 than by Channel 4? **30 min**
5. Which channel televises the most movies? **Channel 4**
6. How many more hours of television programs are shown in the graph for Channel 4 than for Channel 5? **2½ hours**
7. What is the total number of hours that Channel 4 televises sports and movies? **6 hours**
8. What is the total number of hours televised for Channel 5? **7½ hours**
9. Does Channel 5 televise more hours of cartoons and movies or news and sports? **news and sports**
10. Which channel televises more hours of programming? **Channel 4**

Scrambled Shapes

Unscramble the letters in each flower to spell a geometry word. Use the Shape Bank to help you. Then, label the shapes in the Shape Bank.

cylinder
triangle
square
cone
sphere
cube
cube
triangle

Geometry

Shape Bank

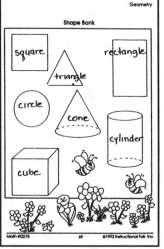

square
triangle
rectangle
circle
cone
cylinder
cube

Geo-Fun

A farmer is trying to design a fence that is 12 square units. On the geoboards below, draw 4 different ways he can build the fence.

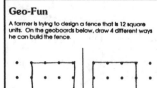

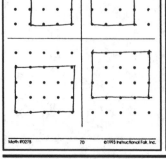

Geometry

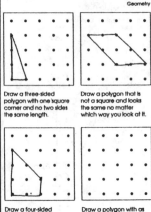

Draw a three-sided polygon with one square corner and no two sides the same length.

Draw a polygon that is not a square and looks the same no matter which way you look at it.

Draw a four-sided polygon with three sides different lengths.

Draw a polygon with as many sides as you want.

Can You Find These?

Geometry

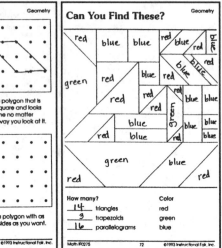

How many?		Color
14	triangles	red
9	trapezoids	green
16	parallelograms	blue

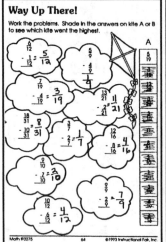

Math IF0275   64   ©1993 Instructional Fair, Inc.
Math IF0275   65   ©1993 Instructional Fair, Inc.
Math IF0275   66   ©1993 Instructional Fair, Inc.
Math IF0275   67   ©1993 Instructional Fair, Inc.
Math IF0275   68   ©1993 Instructional Fair, Inc.
Math IF0275   69   ©1993 Instructional Fair, Inc.
Math IF0275   70   ©1993 Instructional Fair, Inc.
Math IF0275   71   ©1993 Instructional Fair, Inc.
Math IF0275   72   ©1993 Instructional Fair, Inc.

4.
5826
□ □ □
x □
3,410

5.
3459
□ □ □
x □
3,740

6.
8641
□ □
x □ □
1,152

7.
2053
□ □
x □ □
1,600

8.
1968
□ □ □
x □
1,674

9.
2825
□ □
x □ □
2,050

10.
12365
□ □ □ □
x □
4,956

11.
52298
□ □ □ □
x □
41,460

12.
25674
□ □ □
x □ □
33,858

37

©1993 Instructional Fair, Inc.

Division Design

Color in the squares that have numbers divisible by 3, 4 or 7 to form a design.

40	27	10	17	28	23	41	36	70
63	29	1	15	22	45	50	5	12
19	11	16	25	2	5	49	1	10
53	32	11	33	26	32	55	72	29
21	13	43	17	44	31	13	58	18
11	27	23	18	34	77	23	6	17
55	13	8	5	58	19	56	61	37
42	1	23	14	65	21	11	25	35
30	12	37	13	20	61	29	9	24

Put an X on the squares that are divisible by 5.
Put a △ on the squares that are divisible by 2.

30	39	24	37	40	27	16	19	25	47	12	23	5
17	55	11	60	9	15	7	65	3	10	33	35	1
2	29	20	21	32	31	50	29	8	43	45	41	13

Make a design in the grid below. Write the numbers divisible by 5, 7 or 9 in the squares that will form a design. Then, fill in the other squares with numbers that are not divisible by 5, 7 or 9.

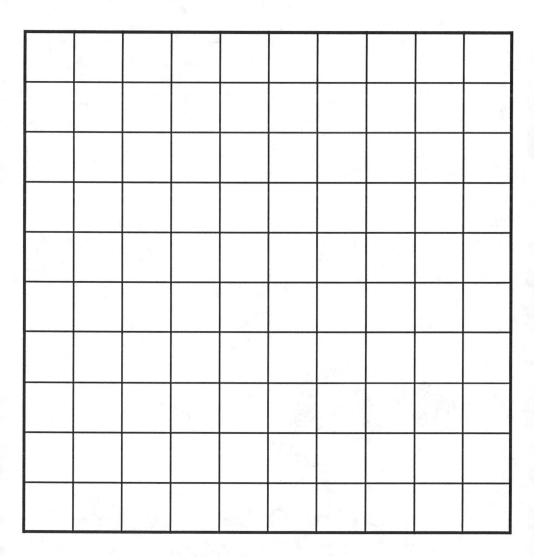

©1993 Instructional Fair, Inc.

Missing Pieces

Fill in the boxes with the missing numbers.

1.
```
       □ 0 4
  7 | 7 2 □
     -7
     ─────
      0 □
      - 0
     ─────
       2 □
     - □ □
     ─────
         0
```

2.
```
      6 □ □
  8 | 4 □ 4 0
    -4 8
    ──────
      0 □
      - 0
    ──────
      4 0
    - □ □
    ──────
        0
```

3.
```
      3 0 □
  9 | 2 □ 7 □
    -2 7
    ──────
      0 □
      - 0
    ──────
      7 2
    - □ □
    ──────
        0
```

4.
```
        7
  5 | 3 □
   - □ □
   ──────
       □
```

5.
```
      □ 2
  7 | 5 0 4
   - □ 9
   ──────
     □ 4
     1 4
   ──────
       □
```

6.
```
      9 □
  4 | 3 □ 4
   - □ □
   ──────
     0 □
     - 4
   ──────
       □
```

40

©1993 Instructional Fair, Inc.

Connect the answers in the order of the problems to find something a detective uses.

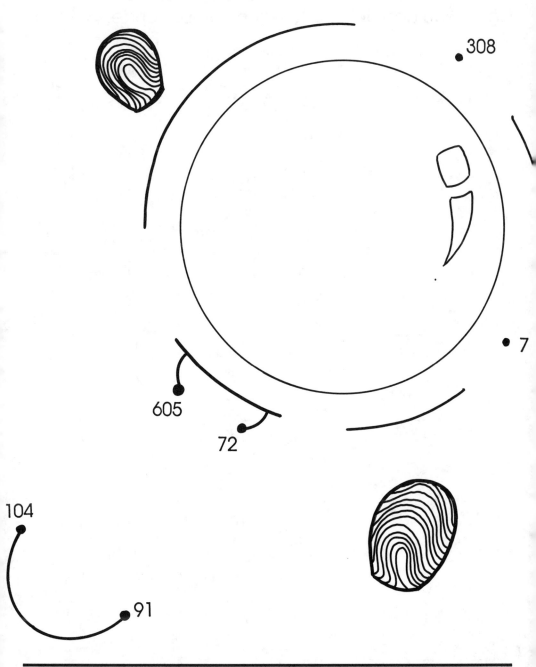

.308

• 7

605

72

104

•91

©1993 Instructional Fair, Inc.

Division in Space

Solve the problems. Then, connect the answers in the order of the problems to make a "space"tacular object! Note: You can only go to each number once.

1. $9\overline{)45}$

2. $5\overline{)15}$

3. $3\overline{)12}$

4. $6\overline{)36}$

5. $3\overline{)21}$

6. $6\overline{)48}$

7. $3\overline{)6}$

8. $3\overline{)27}$

9. $4\overline{)28}$

10. $2\overline{)10}$

11. $9\overline{)36}$

12. $2\overline{)18}$

13. $5\overline{)30}$

14. $6\overline{)18}$

15. $3\overline{)3}$

16. $5\overline{)40}$

17. $4\overline{)16}$

18. $7\overline{)49}$

19. $9\overline{)45}$

20. $8\overline{)72}$

21. $7\overline{)42}$

©1993 Instructional Fair, Inc.

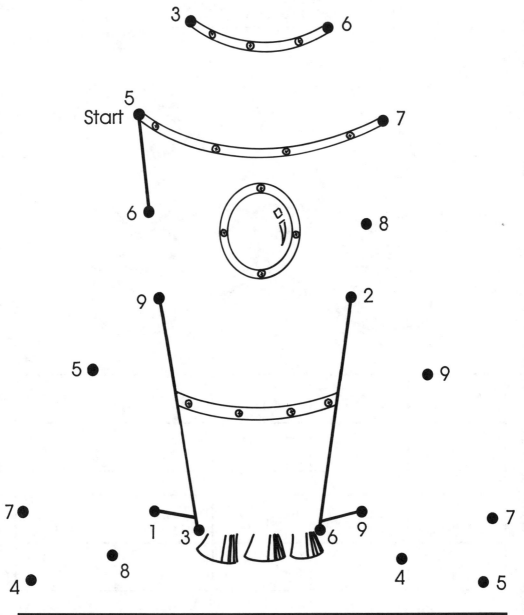

A Fun Riddle

Solve the problems. Then, use the decoder to answer the riddle.

> ## What is black, white and red all over?

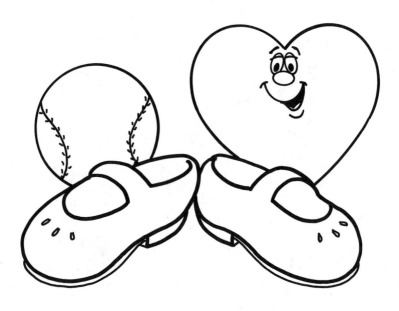

167 R3	308 R2	20 R2	358 R1	205 R2
U	H	A	S	T

7 R2	134 R3	51 R4	314 R3	52 R5
N	R	I	K	W

$7\overline{)142}$

$2\overline{)717}$ $9\overline{)2829}$ $4\overline{)671}$ $5\overline{)37}$ $7\overline{)2201}$

_____   _____   _____   _____   _____

$8\overline{)421}$ $7\overline{)361}$ $3\overline{)617}$ $3\overline{)926}$ $4\overline{)82}$

_____   _____   _____   _____   _____

$5\overline{)673}$ $5\overline{)102}$ $6\overline{)2149}$ $8\overline{)2466}$

_____   _____   _____   _____

45   ©1993 Instructional Fair, Inc.

Math by Design

Solve the problems. Shade in each box that contains
an answer. Write what geometric design you see.

120	111	94	55	419	437
87	210	49	420	24	37
438	112	189	368	195	39
421	67	114	188	190	194
439	124	93	107	369	72

$$35 \times 6 \qquad 47 \times 2$$

$$65 \times 3 \qquad 73 \times 6$$

Design = _____

$$56 \times 2 \qquad 84 \times 5 \qquad 27 \times 7 \qquad 46 \times 8$$

$$5\,\overline{)670} \qquad 7\,\overline{)427}$$

$$2\,\overline{)364} \qquad 4\,\overline{)472}$$

181	123	60	126	64	183
102	134	91	61	97	24
96	62	124	67	103	90
60	182	109	122	118	72
104	92	50	63	20	98

$$8\,\overline{)872} \qquad 6\,\overline{)372}$$

Design = _____

$$5\,\overline{)485} \qquad 9\,\overline{)819} \qquad 3\,\overline{)309} \qquad 8\,\overline{)976}$$

55	937	84	862	57	53
196	140	82	492	342	142
860	672	197	935	195	937
450	234	83	813	861	139
936	812	438	54	448	938

7 ⟌ 980

56
x 8

Design = _____

73
x 6

287
x 3

82
x 6

224
x 3

38
x 9

9 ⟌ 7308

5 ⟌ 975

4 ⟌ 936

6 ⟌ 324

8 ⟌ 656

63
x 7

82
x 7

82	76	302	575	20	442
74	304	441	52	73	48
77	75	306	15	19	305
51	32	49	53	574	37
431	78	573	47	46	23

4 ⟌ 212

6 ⟌ 444

Design = _____

25
x 3

76
x 4

9 ⟌ 135

8 ⟌ 392

©1993 Instructional Fair, Inc.

Solve and Search

Solve the problems below and on page 49. Then, find and circle the answers on the chart on page 49. Answers will be in a straight line, but may be in any direction.

1.
$$356 \times 65$$

2.
$$1892 + 3567$$

3.
$$4562 - 384$$

4.
$$5\overline{)470}$$

5.
$$1495 + 4582$$

6.
$$7\overline{)5896}$$

7.
$$842 \times 25$$

8.
$$2489 - 1956$$

9.
$$4876 + 542$$

10.
$$7\overline{)980}$$

11.
$$9821 - 6154$$

12.
$$645 \times 72$$

13.   9732   14.   984   15.   9 ⟌747
       - 1871   + 76

4	5	9	6	8	2
8	1	3	4	2	3
3	6	7	0	2	1
5	3	6	8	4	4
8	4	5	2	8	0
3	2	1	0	5	0
2	7	4	9	8	1
7	7	0	6	1	0
1	5	4	1	8	6
2	8	6	2	9	0
1	8	3	6	6	7
7	5	9	5	4	5
3	4	6	4	4	0

Find the Sign

Write the correct sign in each circle to make the problem correct.

5 $\bigcirc$ 5 = 25		129 $\bigcirc$ 43 = 3
10 $\bigcirc$ 2 = 12		657 $\bigcirc$ 164 = 493
6 $\bigcirc$ 3 = 18		45 $\bigcirc$ 5 = 225
21 $\bigcirc$ 9 = 12		14 $\bigcirc$ 7 = 98
32 $\bigcirc$ 12 = 20		192 $\bigcirc$ 23 = 215
63 $\bigcirc$ 9 = 7		8 $\bigcirc$ 8 = 64
40 $\bigcirc$ 32 = 72		328 $\bigcirc$ 82 = 4
16 $\bigcirc$ 12 = 192		154 $\bigcirc$ 62 = 92
20 $\bigcirc$ 4 = 5		36 $\bigcirc$ 5 = 31
336 $\bigcirc$ 6 = 56		32 $\bigcirc$ 4 = 8
68 $\bigcirc$ 52 = 120		987 $\bigcirc$ 21 = 47
840 $\bigcirc$ 54 = 786		523 $\bigcirc$ 334 = 857

©1993 Instructional Fair, Inc.

Shaping Up

Use the shapes to solve the problems.

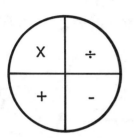

8	96	48
12	6	36
64	51	72

⌐⊔⊓ = _____   ⊔⊔⊃⌐ = _____

⊐⊿⌐ = _____   ⊓⊃⊏ = _____

⊐⊃⌐ = _____   ⊐⊿⌐ = _____

⊏⊔⌐ = _____   ⊐⊔⊏ = _____

⊔⊃□ = _____   ⊐⊿⌐ = _____

⌐⊿⌐⊿⊿□⊔⊐⊐⊏ = _____

Up We Go

Draw a straight line to match each number on the left with its rounded number on the right. Put the letters without lines through them on the blanks on page 53 to spell out a message.

Round to the nearest ten.

Left		Right
45	Ⓡ	80
23	Ⓢ	30
76	Ⓓ Ⓒ	640
482	Ⓤ Ⓞ	60
31	Ⓔ Ⓐ Ⓝ	50
36	Ⓓ Ⓕ	40
642	Ⓝ Ⓔ Ⓣ	480
389	Ⓖ	270
57	Ⓑ Ⓛ	20
267	Ⓢ Ⓘ	1,780
1,782	Ⓞ	390

Round to the nearest hundred.

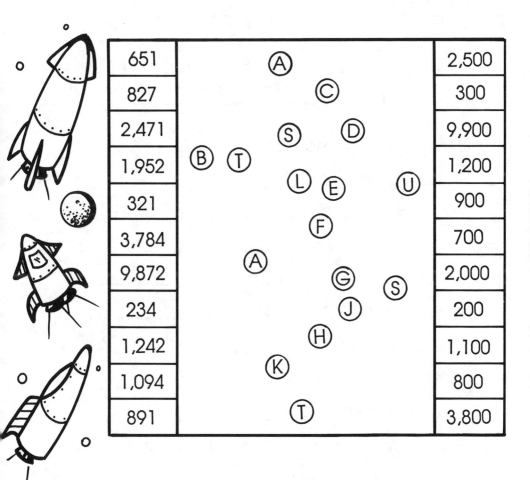

651	Ⓐ	2,500
827	Ⓒ	300
2,471	Ⓢ Ⓓ	9,900
1,952	Ⓑ Ⓣ	1,200
321	Ⓛ Ⓔ Ⓤ	900
3,784	Ⓕ	700
9,872	Ⓐ	2,000
234	Ⓖ Ⓢ	200
1,242	Ⓙ	1,100
1,094	Ⓗ	800
891	Ⓚ	3,800
	Ⓣ	

Decimal Dilemma

Write each decimal. Then, shade in the answers on page 55 to find the answer to this riddle:

> **What are the two favorite letters of children?**

1. six and ninety-one hundredths _____
2. three and five tenths _____
3. eight and twenty-four hundredths _____
4. four and three tenths _____
5. seven and thirty-six hundredths _____
6. eight and eighteen hundredths _____
7. two and one tenth _____
8. sixty and four hundredths _____
9. one hundredth _____
10. thirty-three and thirty-three hundredths _____
11. sixty-four and five tenths _____
12. four and seventy-five hundredths _____
13. nine and four hundredths _____
14. twenty-one and three tenths _____
15. fifty-six and forty-seven hundredths _____
16. seventy and five hundredths _____

8.18 .95 47.5 7.05 .001

3.5 .818 .818 .35 818 35

.01 81.8

.035 73.6 7.36 .736 736 .705

.0736

.691 69.1 70.05 6.91

691

1

.475 .213

90.4 600.4 213

.604 4.75 60.04 9.04 .5647

5.647 .43

2.13 .824 333.3 8.42 2.1 564 .3333

.21 21.3 21 56.47

.645 64.5 .904

6.45 3.333 333 .824 8.2 33.33

4.3

475 645

904 .6004 705 8.24 .1

43

Tic-Tac-Toe with X and O

Solve the problems. Find the answers in the Answer Box and place either an X or an O in the square. Find the tic-tac-toes!

36.14 + 2.63	59.16 + 3.04	7.04 + 3.54
67.50 + 51.04	32.14 + 57.02	82.73 + 27.67
72.4 + 51.3	12.57 + 3.41	89.31 + 43.45

43.67 - 32.98	98.7 - 6.5	72.04 - 3.43
80.54 - 37.62	42.4 - 14.3	24.98 - 9.04
36.72 - 5.98	59.34 - 42.95	82.47 - 3.95

48.32 + 38.49	32.4 + 7.9	67.31 - 51.98
☐	☐	☐
27.51 - 3.95	97.32 + 7.02	55.5 - 4.4
☐	☐	☐
33.04 + 27.93	78.42 - 59.04	61.04 + 5.93
☐	☐	☐

Answer Box

92.2 O	62.20 X	10.69 O	118.54 X	60.97 X
68.61 X	15.98 O	23.56 X	51.1 O	78.52 X	16.39 O
15.94 O	38.77 X	110.40 O	86.81 O	89.16 X
10.58 O	19.38 X	28.1 O	104.34 O	66.97 X	123.7 O
42.92 X	30.74 O	132.76 X	15.33 X	40.3 O

Chow Time

Hamburger			$1.20
with cheese			.20
Hot Dog			$.75
with cheese			.20
with chili			.20
French Fries			$.90
	S	M	L
Soft Drink	$.75	.90	1.20

$ 3.20

Fill in the missing numbers on the chart.

You Had	You Bought	Money Left Over
$3.75	1 cheeseburger 1 French fry 1 medium soft drink	
$1.82	1 chili dog 1 small soft drink	
	1 hamburger 1 cheese dog 1 small soft drink	$.66
	1 hamburger 1 chili cheese dog 2 French fries 1 small soft drink 1 medium soft drink	$.84
$5.96	1 cheeseburger 2 French fries 1 large soft drink	
$4.00		$.70

Fractions of Pizzas

Using the Word Bank, write the fraction of the pizza that has been eaten. Then, circle the answers in the puzzle.

```
T  A  R  F  Q  U  D  P  H  F  O  J  F  H
W  H  B  O  H  J  Y  R  M  Z  F  L  L  T
O  S  R  N  X  T  M  O  I  V  A  G  N  X
T  H  C  E  S  E  R  D  N  H  K  H  I  I
H  T  Q  F  E  D  T  U  E  W  T  P  K  S
I  N  T  I  E  F  V  N  O  U  P  E  Z  E
R  E  W  F  O  R  O  L  F  F  X  L  N  N
D  T  H  T  S  G  F  U  B  L  E  A  E  O
S  X  R  H  Q  A  M  B  R  E  O  N  L  N
I  I  J  S  S  H  T  N  E  T  R  U  O  F
K  S  H  T  F  I  F  E  E  R  H  T  H  C
F  I  V  E  E  I  G  H  T  H  S  S  W  Y
```

Word Bank

two-thirds	one-fifth	six-tenths
three-fourths	one-fourth	one-sixth
five-eighths	whole	four-tenths
one-half	three-fifths	one-third

Wheels of Wonder

Fill in the missing blanks by adding the fractions from the inside out.

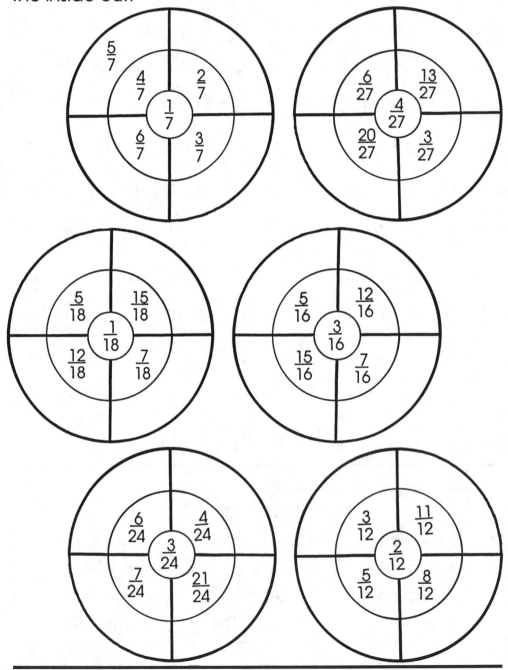

Circle 1 (outer ring: 28ths)

$\dfrac{20}{28}$ $\dfrac{9}{28}$

$\dfrac{13}{28}$

$\dfrac{18}{28}$ $\dfrac{6}{28}$

Circle 2 (48ths)

$\dfrac{5}{48}$ $\dfrac{16}{48}$

$\dfrac{13}{48}$

$\dfrac{31}{48}$ $\dfrac{24}{48}$

Circle 3 (15ths)

$\dfrac{2}{15}$ $\dfrac{4}{15}$

$\dfrac{1}{15}$

$\dfrac{10}{15}$ $\dfrac{7}{15}$

Circle 4 (32nds)

$\dfrac{21}{32}$ $\dfrac{3}{32}$

$\dfrac{5}{32}$

$\dfrac{14}{32}$ $\dfrac{17}{32}$

Circle 5 (92nds)

$\dfrac{65}{92}$ $\dfrac{18}{92}$

$\dfrac{73}{92}$

$\dfrac{54}{92}$ $\dfrac{31}{92}$

Circle 6 (52nds)

$\dfrac{25}{52}$ $\dfrac{5}{52}$

$\dfrac{38}{52}$

$\dfrac{28}{52}$ $\dfrac{31}{52}$

Way Up There!

Work the problems. Shade in the answers on kite A or B to see which kite went the highest.

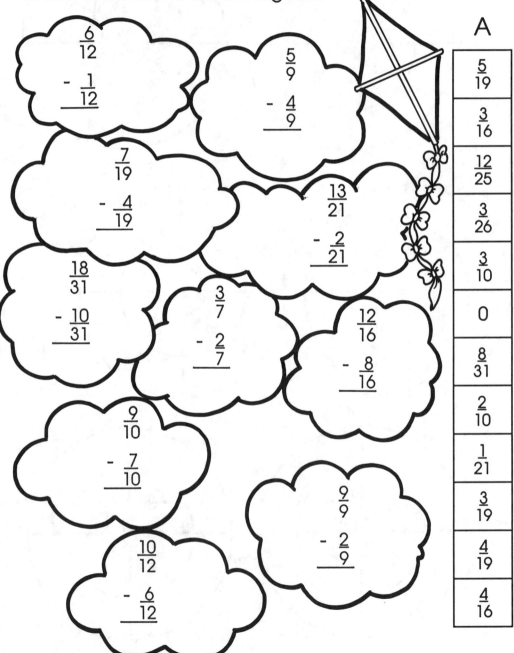

$$\frac{6}{12} - \frac{1}{12}$$

$$\frac{5}{9} - \frac{4}{9}$$

$$\frac{7}{19} - \frac{4}{19}$$

$$\frac{13}{21} - \frac{2}{21}$$

$$\frac{18}{31} - \frac{10}{31}$$

$$\frac{3}{7} - \frac{2}{7}$$

$$\frac{12}{16} - \frac{8}{16}$$

$$\frac{9}{10} - \frac{7}{10}$$

$$\frac{9}{9} - \frac{2}{9}$$

$$\frac{10}{12} - \frac{6}{12}$$

A

$\frac{5}{19}$
$\frac{3}{16}$
$\frac{12}{25}$
$\frac{3}{26}$
$\frac{3}{10}$
0
$\frac{8}{31}$
$\frac{2}{10}$
$\frac{1}{21}$
$\frac{3}{19}$
$\frac{4}{19}$
$\frac{4}{16}$

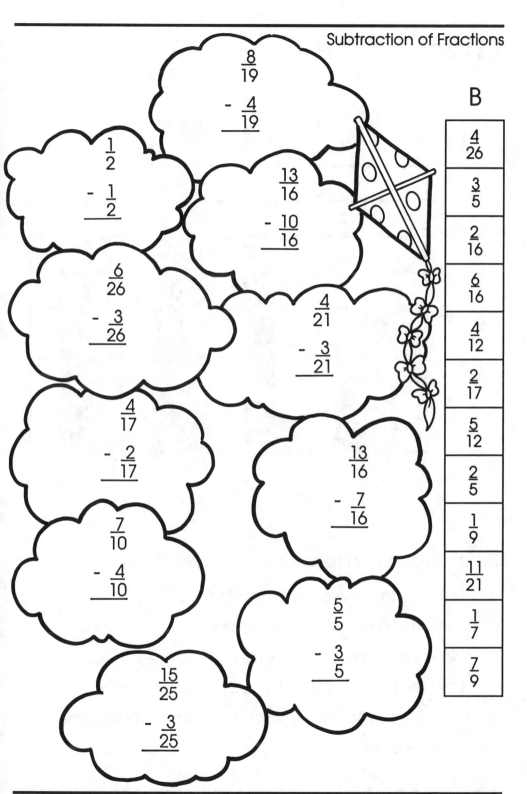

$$\frac{8}{19} - \frac{4}{19}$$

$$\frac{1}{2} - \frac{1}{2}$$

$$\frac{13}{16} - \frac{10}{16}$$

B

$\frac{4}{26}$
$\frac{3}{5}$
$\frac{2}{16}$
$\frac{6}{16}$
$\frac{4}{12}$
$\frac{2}{17}$
$\frac{5}{12}$
$\frac{2}{5}$
$\frac{1}{9}$
$\frac{11}{21}$
$\frac{1}{7}$
$\frac{7}{9}$

$$\frac{6}{26} - \frac{3}{26}$$

$$\frac{4}{21} - \frac{3}{21}$$

$$\frac{4}{17} - \frac{2}{17}$$

$$\frac{13}{16} - \frac{7}{16}$$

$$\frac{7}{10} - \frac{4}{10}$$

$$\frac{5}{5} - \frac{3}{5}$$

$$\frac{15}{25} - \frac{3}{25}$$

65 ©1993 Instructional Fair, Inc.

TV Time

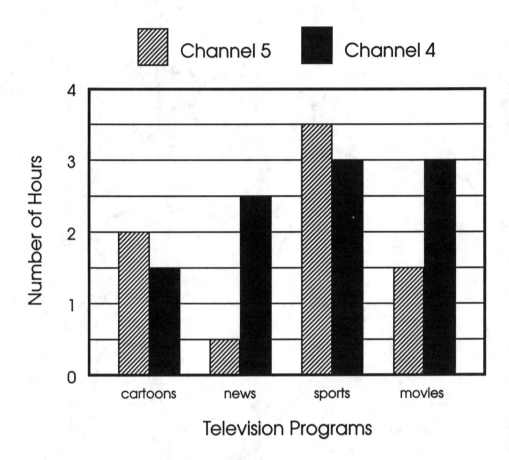

Channel 5   Channel 4

Number of Hours

cartoons   news   sports   movies

Television Programs

Use the bar graph to answer the following questions.

1. How many more hours does Channel 4 deliver televised news than Channel 5? _____

2. How many more hours does Channel 5 televise sports than Channel 4? _____

3. What is the total number of hours that Channel 5 televises news and cartoons? _____

4. How many more minutes of cartoons are televised by Channel 5 than by Channel 4? _____

5. Which channel televises the most movies?

   _____

6. How many more hours of television programs are shown in the graph for Channel 4 than for Channel 5? _____

7. What is the total number of hours that Channel 4 televises sports and movies? _____

8. What is the total number of hours televised for Channel 5? _____

9. Does Channel 5 televise more hours of cartoons and movies or news and sports? _____

   _____

10. Which channel televises more hours of programming? _____

67   ©1993 Instructional Fair, Inc.

Scrambled Shapes

Unscramble the letters in each flower to spell a geometry word. Use the Shape Bank to help you. Then, label the shapes in the Shape Bank.

Shape Bank

69 ©1993 Instructional Fair, Inc.

Geo-Fun

A farmer is trying to design a fence that is 12 square units. On the geoboards below, draw 4 different ways he can build the fence.

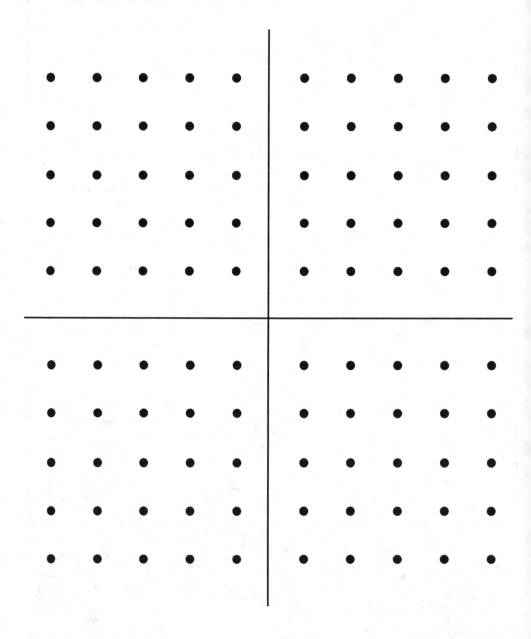

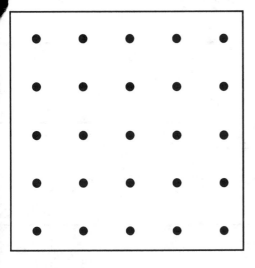

Draw a three-sided polygon with one square corner and no two sides the same length.

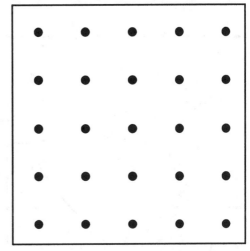

Draw a polygon that is not a square and looks the same no matter which way you look at it.

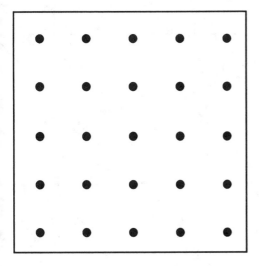

Draw a four-sided polygon with three sides different lengths.

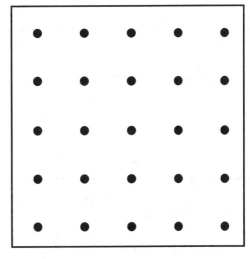

Draw a polygon with as many sides as you want.

 ©1993 Instructional Fair, Inc.

Can You Find These?

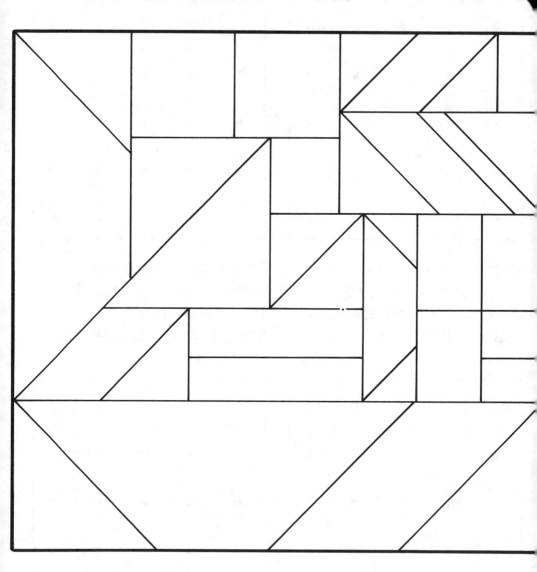

How many?

_____ triangles

_____ trapezoids

_____ parallelograms

Color

red

green

blue

 ©1993 Instructional Fair, Inc.